Sonnets in the key of life

By Carlos Scandiffio

The Autumn of my life

In the Autumn of my life she brings her Spring

The natural freshness of youth in her eyes

Why should I care who or what they sing?

When I am her truth and they bring lies

I know no shame in love unless denied

For in this world we are but all we need

Your touch, your words, your life, your cries

And I will stand in love or on my knees

Her evergreen knows not of age or caste

Why must I thrive for praises every day?

Her love and passion against the odds will last

And should she go I would quickly fade away

I love her Spring as I've loved my every season

Even in the cruelest of winters shines the sun

The clickety-clack of his torn soul

He poured on cotton, curtains drawn

The fact, the fiction, the truth, his all

Were left amidst ink blotches 'til dawn

I loved to listen on rainy days

The clickety-clack and then the bing

As I sat right next to him on my chaise

Like music to my ears it would ring

The crooked "t" and the broken "i"

The poetry of the cotton sheet

The words that would never lie

All in the past, all bittersweet

The clickety-clack of my father's words

Live in my heart forever

Conjure up more grief, I dare you

For I have had my fill of blood and tears

Hoist the colors of your vindictive brood

I shall stand firmly amidst the courage of my fears

If your angels be fair and true to love bestowed

Let them come for me like thieves in the night

As I have witnessed the nefarious signs they bode

When they decimated Babylon to satisfy your plight

I am you as you are me, but yours I'm not

You are made of dying faith and darkened vengeance

Whereas I am purified by your actions which are naught

Neither slave nor servant or hostage to your ascendance

Conjure up more grief if you must, I dare you

For we will meet again in heaven

No natural death for her in this play of life

Only the type Desdemona should endure

No, her moor was not Venetian in the end

For love denied never he would find a cure

Was he right or wrong or did it matter?

More than enough he had given her

But from his mouth for her it was all clatter

As she spiked his heart as with a spur

Deep in her lethargic rest she laid

Her golden hair resting on her face

As her Moorish Captain hovered unafraid

Strong hands wrapped about her nape

But I did not kill her, though she must die

Someone will one day, a bright, glorious day

If winter be winter

If winter be winter when winter comes

I shall seek the warmth of her words back home

For it is her who brings seasons to my tortured heart

She knows about genuine love for love and love alone

I have dallied in the darkness of my twisted mind

In more times and circumstances that I care to speak

She has had faith in me where I had none

And I relished every season she brought me

As I tumble through this life in search of peace

Jaded, old and bruised but full of wonder

She will forever save my Fall with Spring

Set the struggle of my mind and heart asunder

So let that winter come at last

I shall be safe forever in her arms

Only one left dangling from the highest branch

A single solitary ruby shimmering against the sun

Neither wind nor rain or man her skin could reach

Gripping her wooden veins where her life begun

Dazzle me once more from your lofty height

Temptress of love and of love denied

Purge the maladies that in me creep at night

I shall listen faithfully and your will abide

Ah, here comes a gust blowing from the south

Caressing your stem and your leaves alike

And I sit below still feeling the drouth

As my lips rejoice waiting for the bite

Only one left dangling from the branch

Shimmering still against the evening sun

Youth

Dare I touch it only in my dream of peace

Where piety, passion and love were one

Where winds of dissonance were but a breeze

Where the heart was love and of hate had none

Dare I caress it only in my memory

Now that my temper often goes awry

And I so wish to fool time in reverie

And take back what once was mine

My life and loves unremarkable today

As scars of battles past no longer hurt

But the heart tugs and heavy weighs

Struggling with a present cold and curt

Dare I touch it only in my dreams of peace

As I sleep and go back to who I was

Quietly she sat under her beloved Christmas tree

Slowly dying the natural death of love lost

Her tears flowing when the truth became free

As I stood before her amidst the winter frost

Almost all the sounds escaped the room

And memories that had meaning to my life

Did not survive the storm of the impending doom

As her words carved my heart as with a knife

Neither discords, nor remorse, or strife

Appeared to rescue us from the death of love

And in silence she bemoaned the loss of life

As God and the angels cursed me from above

Quietly I sat under our beloved Christmas tree

And there I died my natural death alone

Such a forsaken, rare pleasure of this life

Often abandoned in skirmishes of passion

Herculean efforts to foolishly stand ground

Forgoing that our hearts exceed compassion

Doting lessons from ancestors never perish

If we learned them we must make them perennial

Fools of fortune we become if we don't cherish

Such a sweet eternal peace, albeit ephemeral

In matters of the heart I swim in passion

Letting the fervor and the heat devour me

Of the mind I shall always choose compassion

Marrying my heart with my mind's plea

Such a forsaken, rare pleasure of this life

To be the happiest and swim in passion

Her vilely written verses linger dead and useless

She is devoid of feeling

Aiming at gratuitous fame she is fruitless

She peddles healing

She writes of life and love unknown to her

She is bethrown to darkness

For in the pure light of day she is sour

Her life dreadfully tarnished

She knows the time of penitence will come at last

She will be found wanting

Not by any court in her forsaken illusory land

But a higher power waiting

Her vilely written verses read charmingly

But in her mind, the storm still rages

She called it Paradise but it escaped my eyes

Or perhaps I had lost all will to see

And I called her horizons and her sky a lie

As she sat in love and bleeding by the sea

I went back to the shore a million times

Where she stared at her sky and at her sea

Where she planted her footsteps in the sand

Where the place she had built was just for me

And I saw her ocean and her mangrove trees

And the sun as it caressed her clouds

And the loons gently gliding in the breeze

And the line where the ocean and the sky collide

Ah, to see her Paradise the way she did

As I sat in love and bleeding by the sea

Engrave the grave of love denied

For I have been dragged enough

It matters not the time to bide

Engrave the grave at last

Impending peace is what I seek

Eternal love without the darkness

The kind only a kind hand can give

Engrave the grave to make me harmless

I have lived and loved intensely

With burning ardor and compassion

So lay me down ever so gently

Engrave the grave to keep my passion

Engrave the grave of life well lived

For I have been and now I've passed

Above the treetops and the clouds, the truth lies bare

Like her words to me in the garden of our home

The good, the evil, and all things that should be fair

Will come to me to castoff or to atone

She comes to me in dreams of white

Whispering words of love and mercy

Like a soft breeze as I sleep through the night

Still holding my hand as I complete the journey

And I wonder if she knows how and who I am today

If her love for life and love denied endure

If her spirit lives in me or if I've strayed

If the man she suffered for has matured

She is the truth above the treetops and the clouds

And all the passion and the love that night enshrouds

In the corner of my street I sit at night

Watching them gather beyond street lamps

Behind the sails and trees of Battery park

When the city sleeps along the river banks

Hera, Poseidon, Athena and Apollo

Dance on the grass around the park

And they sing and they prance in the hollow

Always livelier and louder after dark

Vagrants join in the fanfare of sound

And are blessed and enlightened alike

Doubled with laughter, falling on the ground

Barely concealing their human delight

And from the corner of my street I see the sun

As it washes the Gods from the night.

Anon

Anon my good man for the world can wait

Your sweet spouse is not lost to the past

Anon she will save you from those fates

And your love and life will forever last

Anon you shall tell me of your peace

Your discords fading into former life

Your anxious heart and pain will slowly quiesce

Anon you will stare at yourself in her eyes

Anon you will spare your own life for hers

The one blessing of your God to save

Cherish you shall your forthcoming years

Anon you will avoid that lonely, empty grave

Anon my son for the world can wait

Anon until I am gone before you

Eyes wide shut while I was used

You walked the path and smiled through it all

But in the light, your cloak was dark as night

And I winked and thought of you my muse

How I do admire the calculating ice

And its frozen, heartless kiss

Caressing my skin with those eyes

As I took all that I could in my ignorant bliss

There is a place for the likes of you I'm sure

Somewhere beyond ordinary hearts and minds

A place where the breeze is not disguised as shear

A place where men's senses are numb

There will always be eyes wide shut looking at you

Until your own close their lids forever

Demons

Oh... I have danced with them every night and every day

I've mocked him along with the soldiers while I loved him so

From Paradise through cavalry and crucifixion there I
stayed

Watching him bleed my blood until the last deadly blow

You know who I am because you've danced with me

Your hand held mine and in between us, ghosts

Of a thousand years yearning to be free

But we both knew we needed them most

Hide if you must behind your faith and your illusive love

As I continue to walk amongst the ruins with my ghosts

For I prefer their comfort to the one from your vindictive God

The one you lie to on Sundays at the Kingdom Hall

Oh... we have danced with them every night and every day

Pray if you must, but in the end you will be found wanting.

I heard the voice of softer lips in passing

And again I was in love with life

I heard the voice and she was asking

Whether my hope was indeed rife

I could almost touch the softness of those lips

And in my madness I am certain that I tried

But with the breeze that lifts a thousand ships

Her voice and breath altogether flew by

A passing whisper of love I'm told

Robbing but two seconds of my newfound life

But I swear on hope and love behold!

That in those seconds I forgot our strife

I heard the voice from her lips in passing

And again the tug of love denied.

There's this lovely windowsill down my street

Where she would sit and watch the time go by

Unyielding hope captured in her heartbeat

Amidst the sadness buried deep in her eyes

Purposely I walked past that windowsill

Every day as the winter sun went down

As she was slowly dying there still

Silently enduring her thorny crown

And when one summer rose upon my street

I walked once more below her windowsill

Gone in the night, her heart had ceased to beat

And with it my autumn and her spring

There's this lovely windowsill down my street

Where her heart beats for him there still

There you sit in your cloaked sadness

Silently hanging on every word they say

Ignoring that they feed you utter madness

For tomorrow you'll weep what you forgo today

Are your dreams so frail and filled with darkness

That this heart of yours can no longer see truth?

Or perhaps in your quest to keep them harmless

These living ghosts of hate have swallowed you

Awful the day when your mind awakens

The light invading your poor empty heart

The flow of life deep in your veins aching

The love all gone, buried with your past

There you sit in your perpetual sadness

Silently knowing that what they say are lies

Long after the last light is gone

The emptiness of you fills my heart

I purposely wait for the day to be done

To sit alone in our lost Paradise

Would the winds of that hurricane

Blow me back to years gone by

I would go, even though in vain

To swim in love against the tide

For the ocean can cleanse our darkened past

In tears of salt that purify all wounds

The gentle breeze caressing them at last

Amidst the sand where passion abounds

Long after the last vestiges of sun have left

I see you walking besides our wooden path

A heart gone blind

The silent whisper of his life in vain

Passed like a ghost before his eyes

And there he stood staggered at the end

Utterly confused like a lost child

Such a passionate prisoner of his lies

Thoughtlessly wasting years and love denied

Screaming piteous help for a hindered life

To leave no doubt of his injured, bleeding heart

No trace to be found of his insidious mind

Deep in the sea of his lies concealed

And the world around him blind

Of a reality that only God revealed

The silent whisper of his life in vain

As I stood and watch the heart go blind

What dreads must you endure to survive?

Is it yourself or others that you fear?

Don't you know that your love is still alive?

But you deny it while in your bosom sears

When the heat travels through your veins

And you should yield to it in utter freedom

You withdraw behind prejudice in vain

Because your fears pierce you like a needle

You dread the living ghosts around you

But they are dead and yet still walking

Amidst your dreams and life that you once knew

And the feelings that your heart is blocking

What dreads must you endure to survive

That life itself is not worth living

Desert

Wheeling in the winds of twilight

These bushes of a thousand years

Tell me stories of the native blight

Of a land that once was theirs

Skies of hues in orange red

Aroused by clouds of amber

Stitching with ancestry thread

The spirits of those gone under

Opulent southwestern plains

Arresting both the living and the dead

Mystical message through our veins

Stripping away the truth we dread

Wheeling in the winds of twilight

These magic bushes travel proudly

Dusk

We watched the hues of fiery red fill the sky

In titanic struggle to avoid impending darkness

The scattering clouds of the heavens left awry

Remnants of two lives already shattered

Only the stillness of that ocean in the night

The ripples of which caressed our ears gently

Letting us know that we were both still alive

Not for each other and for others barely

We watched the lights in the house at dusk

A refuge that we once thought hallowed

And the wind stripping away the husk

Of our lives lived in vain and now hollow

We watched those hues of fiery red fill the sky

And when the husk was gone, the seed had rotted

Unfaithful

Bathe at night to cleanse your fears

Of yourself for those are the most

And scrub the salt of all those tears

They burn the skin that others toast

Slip yourself beneath the sheets

Lest he wakens for more love

And gently touch him while he sleeps

For guilt demands your curtain call

Preserve silence throughout night

In the morrow all shall be gone

The filth, the passion, and the lie

Awake now cleansed with curtains drawn

Bathe at night in total darkness

Nobody will know, but one

Dreams

Ah! those of spirits dressed in white

Caress the air all around me

Smiling and whispering in flight

Soft to the touch they flee

Veils that float like swollen clouds

Ivory gulls hovering about me

Displacing disgusts of this life

Wiping away my demon's glee

Have you come for me at last?

Do I unfold wings and follow?

Or must I remain in the past

In a station dark and hollow

But no retort is ever uttered

Only the gentle wings' flutter

Babel

One word amongst us we spoke

The hallowed one he had given

Evil discords our peace cloaked

Never again to be forgiven

In the land of Babylon

Where our deception was born

We proclaimed the challenge to our highest Court

But the wiseman took away our words

One word amongst us was spoken

And suddenly there were sundry

Defying fools whose faith was broken

Giving way to confusion running free

One word we spoke

One word for love

In the end

I shall not be found wanting in the end

As I have laid down all precautions with my heart

The fears, the love denied, all deeply rooted hates

Cast aside with every day and every start

I've saved the colors of my tainted life

Nurturing them quietly albeit only in thought

For my own amusement I retold my strife

Lamenting in silence my own Gordish knot

But in the end, I shall not be found wanting

Not for lack of passion, devotion or love

For I have lived with the devil always taunting

And my rescuing angel hovering above

I shall not be found wanting in the end

For in my grave it will not matter

Never a better life you've lived, my dear

Where parasitical skills were so required

Where the body over mind maxim is clear

Where your golden mane would be admired

But I know the likes of you too well

Having myself been victimized by beauty

The deceit that made your poor heart swell

Turning all that you held precious to pity

And the Ides of May have finally come

Collecting on their way past dues of life

Swiftly your beauty appears to crumb

Adding wretchedness and fear to your strife

Never a better life you've lived my dear

Never a better time to pass

Cynthia's Tea

A calming cup of gentle Eau de Nile

Filled with infusion from a distant past

Hues of blueish darkened green

And her love for life at last

Oh how she smiles her trials aside

Clutching tightly at her English cup

The warmth she keeps deeply inside

To fend off discords and the like

Dressing her table with linen and silk

Laden with crumpets and fruitcakes

Carefully placing her sugar and milk

Oh how she loves these treats to bake

Cynthia is not Cynthia without her cup

And day is but a dark night without her

Ah, you women of the ages in quiet suffering!

Your silence has made these men your masters

And your children dart about you asking

Are they going to be like you or their ringmaster?

Cease your perennial household slavery

Lest you forfeit the right to live in happiness

For he will label every word of yours a knavery

So as to preserve his own in all its cockiness

You own the gift of life within your womb

You were the first word we spoke in love

Your breast was the nectar of our bloom

Your peace has always hover like a dove

Ah, you women of the ages in quiet calm

Arise and let us know you have always been alive

A Child

Fiery eyes filled with the innocence of paradise

He walks untroubled

Evil is no match for his innate faith

His world won't crumble

In the distance hide fear, diffidence and hate

He cannot hear them

Heart wild and inviting like an open gate

Fresh life runs through his veins

The path ahead forged by his God

Shall have no hindrances

To neither damage nor tear his shod

Only deliverance

He will know no pause along the way

Except for us

Lost amidst your own fears and tribulations

The spirit wonders alone

Still alive is one thought in your emotions

Find your way home

Whence came you matters not in the end

Awake! Hardly I see you in your grave

Quandaries will derail your faith at every bend

And yet, you must seek the truth you crave

There is a path that I've travelled countless times

A trail of rocky sward and dirty brome

But the effort is well worth the grime

So long as my struggle takes me home

Lost amidst this world of perfidy and pain

I shall always find my way home

Being You

Where would I be if being meant being like you

Devoid my mind of unbridled thought

Exposed my feelings for you to put the shrew

Detached the heart from compassion and hope

Indeed, where would I be should I become you

A wretched soul inside a shell of doubt and hatred

Pariah to the cheerful world I once knew

Immersed solely in the world you have created

No such fate shall await for me at last

While you remain amidst your hopeless lot

This world has awakened from your ill advice

Pity awaits for the misery you brought

Where would I be if being meant being like you?

Immersed in peace but peacefully alone

A sudden storm

Well beyond the reach of capriciously titillating harbor lights

She struggles against stubborn summer gales

At a rate of knots and never fearful of seaworthy fights

Swelling with pride her tightly pulled-hard sails

Up through the hawse-pipes he came up and she respects him

As she yields to his commands and runs the waves

Staring defiantly at the devil and the deep blue grim

As the gales of summer show their deep green salty graves

Devil to pay as the waves wash stem to stern

Never in irons she tacks between brackish swells

Thrashing to reach the land that she so yearns

Hopeful the gales will release her from their spell

Downwind the harbor lights begin to shine again

Today was not the day to pay the devil his dues

Lunar

The doleful cry of the wolves in mild penumbra

Will bestow upon us mortals her white light

'Tis the first one of the year over Alhambra

And the likes of her have never been so bright

So walk out in the fields of open air

Let the breeze caress your skin at last

For tonight there'll be ample sun to bear

As he shines on her face and in your heart

Behind your earth she will be hidden until morn

Rising the tides of the ocean that you love

Lighting your path as you make your way home

As you run with her and the beauty to behold

The howling and the cries in mild penumbra

Will always bring you peace and take you home

Of the life that I've lived I care but a trifle

For is the souls I've met that truly matter

The gentle ones whom my pain abet and stifle

And the wicked ones whom my faith shatter

I've lived for love and blazing passion

And in return at times I seized ill will

But my heart was never turned to ashen

Impermeable through love for their hate to fill

'twas the souls that always brought me peace

And all their trifles and discords I adored

Those precious lessons that would never cease

Would bring the meaning to my errant soul

Of the life that I've lived I care but a trifle

For 'twas the souls that made it all worthwhile

Gone

That sentiment that anchored me to your life

Had long departed to distant places in mine

No longer a prisoner of your daily strife

Other true believers will worship your shrine

No witness exists of the love I've shared

No papers, no songs, no memories at all

But deep in my heart my soul remains bare

Such pride must be yours for bringing the fall

And I, for winking at your obscure charade

Missed the time that I needed to be me

Divine providence will make memories fade

And it has started for at least now I am free

Whatever had anchored me to your life

Has long departed and will never return

What season matters to her peaceful repose?

Neither Owl, nor Robin, or Blackbird of dawn

Could dissuade the beauty underneath her clothes

As she sleeps in peace through the early 'morn

What dreams may come to her at dusk

That her lips speak softly and she smiles

Dare I not arouse her for such would be brusque

Perhaps it's her way to dispense with trials

My eyes still caress her pale, supple skin

Invisible touch that'd provoke a frown

But the dreams within her only yield a grin

Abundant the passion from the peace she's found

What season matters to her peaceful response?

None, for she has all four in her Belgium heart

I hear the sounds of the corner I once knew

Anchored firmly to the confines of my heart

A place where friendship and love forever grew

Before I left them both behind and tore my life apart

All the colors and the smells and all the voices

Overrun me like wave breaking ashore

I clearly see and can almost touch their faces

As the smiles of ages cut right to my core

And the cobblestones echo my gentle youth

With every trolley and every carriage that they feel

Sturdy souls who will only speak the truth

Of my ancestral voices that linger there still

I hear the sounds of the corner that I once knew

The one I will take with me when I finally go

No one shall give you what I have given you

She said in palpable pain

And she meant the words she uttered from her inner soul

Albeit I knew well they were in vain

Non-believer as I was when darkness came

Her words to me were shallow

What a hurt must have been to endure my disdain

When it was I the hollow

Today as I dither in the waves of a different life

Memories haunt my soul

For I've been made to realize that what I had was rife

And she what I needed to be whole

No one shall give me what she had given me

I shall remember this forever more

Doleful the howling yonder by the trees

Like a squealing cry it comes

Piercing roofs and walls and glass with ease

Ripping off tree buds like crumbs

A thousand sails will tear off their bowsprits

For no mariner shall dare its fury defy

And the poor souls who think themselves fit

Shall deal with the devil sitting at the bow

Foolish the man flouting nature's wrath

For its equal has never been known to thee

Yield with utter respect to its fury's path

As clemency rests solely on the sea

Doleful the howling slashing through midship

Do your servant duties and he will decide

Cello Music

Alone she sat by the window at the store

Staring into space with her usual careless flair

Cascading shinny gold plummeting to the floor

And I, so close that I could almost touch her hair

I stood in silence as the cello filled my senses

And I remembered every minute of every day

The sandy beach, the hurricane, the broken fences

Every twist of love and pain that had made me stay

I took long, slow steps towards the door

I dared not turn around to touch her hair

The heart dragging painfully while I scuffed the floor

And that pleasing, familiar perfume filled the air

There she stayed by the window at the store

Never seeing me, never speaking, never more

Whitish Roses

She's arranged the hues of whitish petals

On the sideboard by the door

Dreams of snow when the storm settles

And crystal flakes turn to hoar

How she adores midwinter whitish roses

As the candle flame shines through

Exclusively in the twilight as the day closes

While they wait for morning dew

Wish I were a stem or bud or petal

To sense the purest of her love

I'll be content to watch her gentle stare

For watching love is far above

She goes about arranging whitish roses

As my heart could not wish more

Filtering through branches, shrubberies and mist

It strikes me blind

What beauty trying to escape the midst

Of earth and heaven intertwined

It warms my skin and heart from farther

Why is this peace so strong?

That I should feel protected through the woods

And fear not moving along?

This is no sun, or nature, or trickery of man

For I'm well verse in those and more

This is the type of peace unlike I have ever seen

Or sensed ever before

I see the purpose of the strike and what it bodes

Meeting my maker at last at the end of the road

Crystalline beauties of champagne and white

Shower the sky with untainted ancient teardrops

The purest heart of nature dressed in bright

Cloaking any pain with glowing, misty raindrops

One rests alone upon the sand by the pier

Winter waves bathe her in salt and withdraw

Never invading the shield of her shell

The sun always present her ice drops to thaw

And I, staring in silence and utterly mystified

In awe of this beauty of champagne and white

Or perhaps a black one if God so decides

Quietly marveled I shall remain 'til the sun alights

Crystalline beauties staring at the sun

As I wait for them to gleam in my eyes

You speak of it amidst your darkest thoughts

Preach no more

You sing your claims of love for naught

Cease your song

Step aside and let reality take its course

Walk no further

You love is dark, your speech is coarse

Speak no longer

Your love as hollow as an empty vessel

Love no more

Your mind as tortured as the hate it nestles

Cease your thoughts

You speak of faith amidst your darkest thoughts

Mystic that you are, lie no more

Oh sweltering Summer amid Nadder Valley

That I should find refuge in a bottle shop

The one perched on High Street just across my alley

The finest in Wiltshire for bitter or stout

My dreams torn apart like Old Wardour Castle

Rolling downland through the Cranborne Chase

No boulders or gullies to bring any hassle

Only flocks of sheep the grassland to grace

Such miniscule hamlet of abundant harmony

With this briefest season of green grass and gold

Embracing millennia from Mere to Salisbury

And such crystal skies my mind to behold

No sweltering summer in the Nadder Valley

As I glance High street from my bottle shop

How can you peddle your trade amongst the desperate?

When your own house is troubled to its very core

Can't you see the weaknesses in their errand spirits?

Is your heart so frigid that you thirst for gore?

I've known you forever and your kin in crime

Your deceitful souls exploiting the dark

And yet, you seek solace amid your own grime

And wipe with your tail what you write in sand

Alas! the pour, gentle souls hoping love from lies

Blind to the scoundrels who pretend knowledge of life

Shall remain alone and lost with their love denied

As you bask in the sun of your murky paradise

How can you peddle your trade amongst the desperate

When your own compassion has died long ago

www.ingramcontent.com/pod-product-compliance
Lightning Source LLC
Chambersburg PA
CBHW081401160726
48000CB00010B/3433